WORLD'S LONGEST-LIVING ANIMALS

80-YEAR-OLD FLAMINGOS!

By Joni Kelly

Please visit our website, www.garethstevens.com. For a free color catalog of all our high-quality books, call toll free 1-800-542-2595 or fax 1-877-542-2596.

Cataloging-in-Publication Data

Names: Kelly, Joni.
Title: 80-year-old flamingos! / Joni Kelly.
Description: New York : Gareth Stevens Publishing, 2019. | Series: World's longest-living animals | Includes index.
Identifiers: LCCN ISBN 9781538216798 (pbk.) | ISBN 9781538216781 (library bound) | ISBN 9781538216804 (6 pack)
Subjects: LCSH: Flamingos–Juvenile literature.
Classification: LCC QL696.C56 K45 2019 | DDC 598.3'5–dc23

Published in 2019 by
Gareth Stevens Publishing
111 East 14th Street, Suite 349
New York, NY 10003

Designer: Andrea Davison-Bartolotta and Laura Bowen
Editor: Joan Stoaltman

Photo credits: Cover, p. 1 Glenn Bartley/All Canada Photos/Getty Images; pp. 2–24 (background) Dmitrieva Olga/Shutterstock.com; p. 7 Marten_House/Shutterstock.com; p. 9 Stephaniellen/Shutterstock.com; p. 11 Kirill Dorofeev/Shutterstock.com; p. 13 Peter Byrne/PA Images/Getty Images; p. 15 Kevin/Wikimedia Commons; p.17 Cloudia Spinner/Shutterstock.com; p. 19 Brieg/Wikimedia Commons; p. 21 Vladimir Wrangel/Shutterstock.com.

Printed in the United States of America

CPSIA compliance information: Batch #CS18GS: For further information contact Gareth Stevens, New York, New York at 1-800-542-2595.

CONTENTS

Boldface words appear in the glossary.

Popular Pink Plumes

Flamingos are one of the most popular birds on Earth! Their pink plumes, or feathers, sticklike legs, and long necks are known by many. They live near the **equator**, where it is hot and wet. But you can see flamingos at zoos all over the world!

WHERE FLAMINGOS LIVE

Greenland

Europe

North America

Asia

Atlantic Ocean

Africa

equator

South America

Indian Ocean

Pacific Ocean

flamingo range

A Wild Life

In the wild, flamingos live for about 20 to 30 years. Some people say they can even live 40 years in the wild. That's pretty long for a bird! Flamingos can only live long if they have enough food and water.

Living Long

Flamingos are great swimmers and fliers. Male and female flamingos take turns keeping their nest and egg safe and feeding their young. This helps their young **survive**! Flamingos even have ways to stay warm in the cold. All these tricks help flamingos live long.

Safety in Numbers

The best way flamingos keep safe is by sticking together in groups called flocks. This allows some to search for food while others look out for predators. Flocks can have a **million** flamingos, though 40,000 is more likely!

Living Even Longer!

Like many birds, flamingos live much longer in **captivity**—as long as 50 to 80 years, in fact! In a zoo, **refuge**, or wildlife park, there are no predators or hunters. Flamingos can receive **medicine**. Plus, there's always plenty of food!

ZOOLOGICAL GARDENS
CHESTER

Greater: The Greatest

The longest-living flamingo in history was Greater! Greater was 5 feet (1.5 m) tall when its head was raised and was the star of the Adelaide Zoo in Australia for many years. Greater was the last of its species, or kind, in all of Australia.

GREATER

From 1933 to 2014, Greater often came up to visitors to greet them. There aren't any records of Greater's birth, so it's hard to know an exact age. When Greater died in 2014, the zoo guessed that Greater was around 83 years old!

GREATER

Chile: A Fine Feathered Friend

Once Greater died, there was only one flamingo left in Australia. Laws stop new flamingos from coming into Australia. Chile turned 75 in 2017. Flamingos are social animals, so zookeepers put a **mirror** in Chile's living space to keep it from being lonely.

CHILE

How to Have Flamingos Forever

Climate change has caused some flamingos to change where they live. It also causes killer storms. Since flamingos only have one egg at a time, these storms hurt the size of a flock for years. Hopefully you can visit one of these beautiful birds soon!

GLOSSARY

captivity: the state of being kept in a place and not being able to leave

climate change: long-term change in Earth's weather, caused partly by human activities

equator: an imaginary line around Earth that is the same distance from the North and South Poles

medicine: a drug taken to make a sick person or animal well

million: the number 1,000,000

mirror: a piece of glass that shows a likeness of what is in front of it

refuge: a place set aside for wild animals to live safely

survive: to live through something

FOR MORE INFORMATION

BOOKS

Borgert-Spaniol, Megan. *Flamingos.* Minneapolis, MN: Bellwether Media, 2014.

Gibbs, Maddie. *Flamingos.* New York, NY: PowerKids Press, 2011.

McCarthy, Cecilia Pinto. *Flamingos.* Mankato, MN: Capstone Press, 2012

WEBSITES

Flamingo
kids.nationalgeographic.com/animals/flamingo/#flamingo-flying.jpg
Read all about flamingos here!

Flamingo Facts
softschools.com/facts/animals/flamingo_facts/5/
If you want to know more about flamingos, read this page!

Flamingo Facts for Kids
coolkidfacts.com/flamingo-facts-for-kids/
Find out some amazing facts about these beautiful, pink birds!

INDEX